Bringing Your Best to Whatever You Do

CAREER, RELATIONSHIPS, LIFE

by Dr. Lashun Bland, DBA

© Copyright 2025 - All rights reserved.

The content contained within this book may not be reproduced, duplicated or transmitted without direct written permission from the author or the publisher.

Under no circumstances will any blame or legal responsibility be held against the publisher, or author, for any damages, reparation, or monetary loss due to the information contained within this book, either directly or indirectly.

Legal Notice:

This book is copyright-protected. It is only for personal use. You cannot amend, distribute, sell, use, quote or paraphrase any part, or the content within this book, without the consent of the author or publisher.

Disclaimer Notice:

Please note the information contained within this document is for educational and entertainment purposes only. All effort has been executed to present accurate, up to date, reliable, complete information. No warranties of any kind are declared or implied. Readers acknowledge that the author is not engaged in the rendering of legal, financial, medical or professional advice. The content within this book has been derived from various sources. Please consult a licensed professional before attempting any techniques outlined in this book.

By reading this document, the reader agrees that under no circumstances is the author responsible for any losses, direct or indirect, that are incurred as a result of the use of the information contained within this document, including, but not limited to, errors, omissions, or inaccuracies.

Contents

Dedication 5

Preface 9

Introduction: My Journey 10

Understanding Success 13

    What Is Success? 14

The Five Steps to Success 16

    Step #1: Be 100 Percent Responsible for Your Own Life 17

    Step #2: Discover What You Want 25

    The Cost of Not Knowing What You Want 34

    What I Wish I'd Known at Thirty 35

    The Permission You're Waiting For 35

    Step #3: Align Your Goals with Your Passion and Purpose ... 38

    Step #4: Believe That You Can 56

    Step #5: Die on the Treadmill 67

Your Journey—Practical Application 82

Moment of Reflection: How You Get Inspired 82

Let's Continue the Journey: Walking Through the Five Steps 83

Step #1 Exercises: 100 Percent Responsible...................................84

Step #2 Exercises: Your Turn—What Do You Really Want? 89

Step #3 Exercises: Align Your Goals with Passion and Purpose 93

Moment of Reflection: How Do You Desire to Express Yourself? 103

Step #4 Exercises: Why Not You? 104

Step #5 Exercises: Die on a Treadmill 113

Creating Your Plan 118

Setting Goals for Success 118

Using Your Monthly Calendar 120

Conclusion: Your Journey Begins Now 125

The Five Steps Revisited..126

About the Author 130

Dedication

To my father, who taught me that facing the truth is the first step to freedom.

To my mother, without whom the journey would have been much harder. To my brother, whose memory reminds me that life is too short not to live fully.

And to my son, my greatest reason to bring my best to whatever I do.

Our deepest fear is not that we are inadequate.

Our deepest fear is that we are powerful beyond measure ...

—*Marianne Williamson, "Our Deepest Fear"*

Preface

Whenever I read Marianne Williamson's poem "Our Deepest Fear," I feel powerful. When I'm struggling with a challenge, I recite it to myself. I ask:

Who am I not to be great? Then I know I can be, and I push forward. Being your best self is possible, though challenging at times. The hardest part is knowing where to begin and how to keep progressing. With the trials and triumphs of daily life, it's easy to lose sight of who you are. One day, you're driven and determined to excel, and the next, you look up and realize you're right where you were a year ago.

This book will help you uncover who you truly are, unlock what you genuinely want, and equip you with tools to boldly chase the life you were meant to live.

Introduction: My Journey

Today, I hold my highest educational achievement—a Doctorate of Business Administration. It's more than a title. It's a testament to years of relentless effort, sacrifice, and an unshakable belief that growth is always within reach. The path wasn't easy. It was marked by long nights of research, countless revisions, moments of doubt, and the constant juggle between academic rigor and personal responsibility. There were times I questioned my capacity to continue, when challenges made me wonder if the finish line was even worth crossing. But every obstacle reminded me of my purpose: to break barriers, set a new standard for myself, and show others what's possible when you refuse to give up. This degree represents more than academic success—it symbolizes resilience. It reflects every moment I chose discipline over comfort, vision over fear, and action over hesitation.

But it wasn't always this way.

When I graduated from high school, I barely passed with a C average—not because I was incapable, but because I didn't know then what I know now. I didn't know how to push myself. I couldn't envision what I wanted in life and didn't understand how each decision would influence my future.

Around age twenty-three, I found myself sitting in my bed in my studio apartment, preparing to get up, get dressed, and go to another day at what I called a "mediocre" job doing mundane work. I knew I didn't want to feel as if I had no purpose. I no longer wanted to simply exist—I wanted to live.

So in that moment, I decided to pursue more knowledge so that more doors of opportunity would open for me. I wanted to be a college graduate and have a meaningful career. Yet I thought to myself: *Where do I start? How am I going to do that? Can I be successful?*

Something inside me said, *Yes. Yes, you can.*

The tools in this book aren't just ideas—they're the exact strategies I used to transform my life. Through focused journaling and strategic planning, I carved a path to where I am today. Now it's your turn to take action and build the future you deserve.

While reading this book, you'll take charge of your growth by writing down your thoughts, evaluating your goals, setting clear weekly and monthly targets, practicing powerful self-reflection, and building a step-by-step roadmap to the life you're ready to create.

This book is crafted to ignite your potential and guide you in becoming the best version of yourself—whatever that vision looks like—and to empower you to turn that vision into reality.

Understanding Success

"Don't aim at success. For success, like happiness, cannot be pursued; it must ensue, and it only does so as the unintended side-effect of one's dedication." —Viktor E. Frankl, Man's Search for Meaning

What Is Success?

Dictionary definition: The accomplishment of an aim or purpose; the attainment of fame, wealth, or social status; a person or thing that achieves desired aims or attains fame.

I define success differently: bringing your best to whatever you do. Whether you complete the task or not, success lies in trying your best. The accomplishment is more frequently the result of being your best.

Now, I don't know about you, but fame isn't one of my aspirations. Yet I believe that, famous or not, I can be successful. Whether or not you decide to become famous and have your star on Hollywood Boulevard, start your own business, or become a fitness expert, you must have a clear definition of what success means to you.

This book is designed to help you decide what that is, centered around the framework I used to achieve my own definition of success. I discovered success in confidence and resilience. I learned that no matter what task I aimed to complete, if I put my all into it, I was successful.

Viktor Frankl's quote crystallized something for me: my definition of success aligned with what I needed most.

The Five Steps to Success

As an adult, I became an avid reader. Through my readings, I distilled what I define as the five steps to success. I hope you can use this framework to bring your best to whatever you do.

Step #1: Be 100 Percent Responsible for Your Own Life

You may be thinking, *"I am, aren't I? I've chosen where I live, where I work, who I live with, and what I like to do for fun."* You may have, yet we all need to admit at some point that others have influenced where we are, whether on purpose or not.

Owning 100 percent of your choices is empowering. Aligning your actions, mindset, and results is where real growth happens. There is freedom in taking complete ownership of your life.

I can hear you now: *"But my dog died." "But my mother never loved me." "But my spouse cheated on me."* I understand. We can't always control what happens to us, but we are fully responsible for how we react and what we do next. That's the part we own completely.

The Foreclosure Letter That Changed Everything

At twenty-four, I bought my first home. I was so proud—a homeowner before twenty-five! I had a job I loved, owned a reliable car, and felt like I was finally "making it." Life was good.

Then I was laid off.

The new position I found didn't pay nearly as much. Suddenly, the mortgage that felt manageable became a burden. The car note that seemed reasonable started to squeeze. I was behind on bills within months.

But here's the part I'm not proud of: I knew I was in trouble, and I did nothing. Instead of facing it, I ignored it. I stopped opening bills. I stopped checking my bank account. I went through life pretending everything was fine. I still went out to dinner with friends. I still hit the bars on weekends. I still shopped for things I didn't need. If you had seen me, you'd never have known I was drowning financially.

I told myself stories: *"It'll work itself out." "I'll catch up next month." "This is just temporary."* I was blaming the layoff. Blaming the new job for not paying enough. Blaming the economy. Blaming everything except the person making the decisions— me.

Then one day, a letter came in the mail.

FORECLOSURE.

My hands shook as I read it. The word felt unreal. People my age didn't get foreclosure notices. That happened to other people, people who made bad decisions, people who weren't responsible. Not me.

Except it was me.

I called my dad, my voice cracking. When I told him I was about to lose my house, there was a long silence on the phone.

"You're about to lose your house?" he repeated, disbelief in his voice. "How did it get this far?"

I had no answer. Just excuses.

He drove over that evening and sat me down at my kitchen table—the same table I was about to lose. He handed me a pen and paper.

"Write down all your bills," he said. "Every single one. When they're due. How much."

I wrote them down, my stomach sinking with each line.

"Now write down how much you make." I wrote down my paychecks.

He pointed at the two columns. "You see this? Your expenses are higher than your income. You have two choices: get rid of the house and car, or make more money." It was that simple. That brutally simple.

The truth I'd been avoiding was right there in black and white. This wasn't the layoff's fault. This wasn't the new job's fault. This was my spending, my avoidance, my refusal to face reality.

"I don't want to get rid of anything," I said quietly.

"Then you need more income," he replied. "And you need it now."

That night, I started looking for a second job. Within a week, I was waitressing. Let that sink in for a moment. I went from being a supervisor managing more than fifteen direct reports at an insurance audit firm, to a billing auditor at a dental insurance company, to a waitress carrying plates and refilling drinks. My ego screamed at me. My college-educated self wanted to be embarrassed. But my "about to lose everything" self? She showed up to every shift. I worked both jobs. I saw my paycheck grow. I watched my bills get paid. For the first time in months, I wasn't drowning—I was swimming.

Then I got a third job.

You might think that's extreme. But here's what I realized: I never wanted to feel that low again. I never wanted to see another foreclosure letter. I never wanted to lie to myself that everything was fine when it wasn't.

I worked three jobs for over a year. I saved my house. I caught up on my car. I built an emergency fund. More importantly, I learned the most valuable lesson of my life:

I am 100 percent responsible for my life.

Not my circumstances. Not the economy. Not my employer. Me.

The layoff happened to me. But the financial crisis? That was on me. I chose to avoid bills. I chose to keep spending. I chose to pretend everything was fine.

And once I stopped blaming and started owning, everything changed. Could I have blamed the layoff and let the house go? Absolutely. Would people have understood? Sure. But would that have made me responsible for my life? No.

Taking 100 percent responsibility isn't about never having setbacks.

- It's about owning your response to setbacks.
- It's about looking at that foreclosure letter and saying, "This is my problem, and I'm going to fix it."
- It's about working three jobs when your pride says you should only need one.
- It's about facing the numbers on the page instead of throwing the bills in a drawer.
- It's about asking for help when you need it—even when it's humbling to make that call to your dad.

That foreclosure letter could have been the end of my homeownership at age twenty-four. Instead, it became the beginning of me taking control of my life. Not just my finances—my entire life. Because once you truly take 100 percent responsibility in one area, you start to see where else you've been making excuses. Where else you've been blaming. Where else you've been avoiding.

And that's when real transformation begins.

Step #2:

Discover What You Want

What do you want? When I say that, I always think of the famous scene from *The Notebook*, where Noah asks Allie, "What do you want?" He begins with "Would you stop thinking about what everyone wants? Stop thinking about what I want, what he wants, what your parents want? What do you want? Allie was experiencing an emotional struggle between her love for Noah and what others wanted for her life. Noah repeatedly asks her at least three times, before Allie replies, "I have to go," and then walks away.

We all experience this. We struggle to make decisions, fearing what others will think or how we'll make someone feel once we decide. In most cases, we don't think about what we actually want.

Take time to get honest with yourself. If you don't define what you want, other factors will do it for you. You've heard the saying, "Life happens." I'm here to tell you, yes, it does. But discovering what you want and living in that can release so much stress and tension. It allows you to think clearly and feel empowered. Clarity and empowerment open opportunities for you to bring your best to whatever you do.

When Grief Made My Decisions for Me

At thirty I thought I had it all figured out. I had a good job, owned my home, was working toward my bachelor's degree, and had an active social life. The single life was fun—nights out with friends, freedom to make my own choices, no one to answer to. I was content. Happy even.

Then I met him. Dating was easy, comfortable. But I wasn't in a rush to change my life. Marriage and children were "someday" things, not urgent needs.

Then my world shattered.

I lost my younger brother.

If you've never experienced sudden, devastating grief, it's hard to explain how it rewrites everything. The person you were before? Gone. Your priorities? Scrambled. Your sense of what matters? Completely transformed.

One day, you're living your life, making plans, thinking you have time. The next day, time feels like a luxury you can no longer trust.

In my grief, something shifted violently inside me. Suddenly, the single life I'd been enjoying felt empty. The career I was building felt meaningless. The partying felt hollow.

I became consumed with a new, urgent thought: I need to create a family. I need something permanent. I need to build something that death can't take away.

Marriage and children went from "someday" to "right now."

Looking back, I can see it clearly: *I wasn't discovering what I wanted. I was running from what I'd lost.*

The decision to marry him was easy. Too easy.

He was there. He was stable. He was willing. And in that moment, anything that promised happiness felt like a lifeline, and I grabbed it with both hands.

I didn't ask myself the hard questions:

- *Do I want to marry him, or do I just want to be married?*
- *Am I choosing this life, or am I running from pain?*
- *Is this what I truly want, or is it what I think will fix how I feel?*

I didn't take time to heal. I didn't take time to process my grief. I didn't take time to rediscover who I was after such profound loss.

I just said yes.

Let me be clear: I don't regret my marriage. How could I? It gave me my son, who is the absolute center of my universe. He is joy personified, and I would walk through that pain a thousand times to have him in my life.

But if I'm being honest—and that's what this book is about—I can also say this: *I shouldn't have gotten married at that time.* Not because he was wrong for me, but because *I wasn't right for myself yet.*

I was broken, grieving, and searching for something to fill the void. That's not the foundation for choosing a life partner. That's not the clarity you need to make one of the biggest decisions of your life.

But I didn't know that then. All I knew was that I was in pain, and marriage promised relief.

What happened next was predictable, though I couldn't see it at the time. I set aside everything I'd been working toward—my career ambitions, my academic goals, my personal dreams. I poured myself into being the perfect wife and devoted mother.

I told myself: *This is what I want now. This is what matters.*

I cooked. I cleaned. I organized. I supported. I sacrificed. I showed up. I gave everything I had to making the marriage work and raising my son with love.

And it still wasn't enough.

The marriage struggled. We struggled. No matter how much I gave, how much I tried, how much I bent myself into the shape of what I thought a wife should be, it wasn't enough to keep us together.

The painful truth I eventually faced: *You can't save a marriage by losing yourself.*

I had become so focused on being what I thought everyone needed me to be that I forgot to ask: *What do I need? What do I want? Who am I beyond this role?*

I had a choice to make: stay in a marriage that was slowly erasing me, or walk away and rediscover myself.

I chose to walk away.

Not because I didn't care. Not because I didn't try. But because I finally realized: *I had never really asked myself what I wanted.*

At age thirty, I thought I wanted what grief told me I wanted. In my marriage, I thought I wanted what society told me I should want. But neither of those wants were truly mine.

They were reactions. Responses. Attempts to fill a void or meet an expectation. They weren't authentic desires born from a clear understanding of who I was and what would fulfill me.

Walking away wasn't easy. It was terrifying, actually.

I was a mother now. I had responsibilities. I had a child who depended on me. What if I was making a mistake? What if I regretted it? What if I ended up alone?

But staying felt like slow suffocation. Like disappearing a little more each day. So I left. And I'm glad I did. Not because the marriage was terrible. Not because he was a bad person. But because *I needed to find myself again.*

I needed to sit with the question I'd been avoiding since I was thirty years old:

What do I actually want?

Not what grief wants. Not what society expects. Not what will make others happy or keep the peace or look good from the outside. What do *I* want?

Here's what I discovered in that season of rediscovery:

- I wanted to finish my education—not because I had to, but because learning lit me up inside.
- I wanted to build a career that mattered—not to prove anything, but because meaningful work fulfilled me.
- I wanted to show my son what it looks like to pursue your dreams even when life gets hard—not by telling him, but by living it.
- I wanted to be whole, not just functional; present, not just performing.

These desires had always been there. But I'd buried them under layers of grief, obligation, and other people's expectations. It took walking away from what I thought I was supposed to want to finally discover what I actually wanted.

The Truth about Discovering What You Want

Here's what no one tells you: Sometimes you have to discover what you DON'T want first.

I didn't want to lose myself in a role.

I didn't want to make major life decisions from a place of pain.

I didn't want to live a life that looked good but felt empty. I didn't want to be so busy being what everyone needed that I forgot who I was.

Those "don't wants" eventually led me to clarity about my real wants:

I want autonomy over my life.

I want to pursue growth without apology.

I want my son to see a mother who honors herself.

I want relationships built on authentic connection, not need or obligation.

I want to bring my best to whatever I do—and that requires knowing what I actually want to do.

The Cost of Not Knowing What You Want

Let me be brutally honest about what it cost me to not ask "What do I want?" sooner:

Years. Years of my life spent on a path that wasn't truly mine.

Energy. Energy poured into sustaining something that was never aligned with my authentic self.

Growth. Growth I delayed because I was too busy being who I thought I should be.

Could I have avoided this? Maybe. If I'd taken time after my brother's death to grieve properly. If I'd sat with the pain instead of running toward anything that promised relief. If I'd asked myself hard questions before making life altering decisions.

But I didn't. And that's okay. Because that detour taught me something invaluable:

You can't skip the work of knowing yourself.

Not for anyone. Not for any reason. Not even for love.

What I Wish I'd Known at Thirty

If I could go back and talk to my thirty-year-old self, grieving and grasping for stability, here's what I'd say:

I know you're in pain. I know you want the hurt to stop. I know marriage and family feel like the answer right now. But before you say yes to anything permanent, ask yourself:

"Am I choosing this because I genuinely want it?"
"Or am I choosing it because I'm afraid, lonely, or hurting?"
"If this wasn't here, what would I be doing with my life?"
"Who am I when I'm not trying to be what someone else needs?"

Take time. Heal. Sit with the discomfort of not having all the answers. Because the cost of making major life decisions before you know what you want isn't just a wrong choice—it's losing years of your life to someone else's script.

The Permission You're Waiting For

You might be waiting for permission to want something different than what you've been choosing. *Consider this your permission:*

You're allowed to want something different than you wanted five years ago.

You're allowed to realize you made decisions from pain, not clarity. You're allowed to walk away from paths that aren't yours—even if you started down them with good intentions.

You're allowed to disappoint people by choosing yourself. You're allowed to say, "I thought I wanted this, but I don't anymore."

That's not failure. That's growth.

That's not being selfish. That's being honest.

That's not giving up. That's waking up.

I walked away from my marriage and walked toward myself. It was the hardest, scariest, best decision I ever made. Not because marriage is wrong, but because *that* marriage wasn't aligned with who I truly was and what I truly wanted. And once I got clear on what I wanted—not what grief wanted, not what looked right, not what was expected—everything changed.

I finished my degree. Then another. Then another.

I built a career that feeds my soul, not just my bank account.

I showed my son what it means to choose yourself even when it's hard.

I became whole.

Now it's your turn.

Stop running from pain or toward relief.

Stop choosing what looks good or what others expect.

Stop living someone else's version of your life.

Sit with the question: *What do I want?*

And then, have the courage to choose it.

Step #3:
Align Your Goals with Your Passion and Purpose

Ask yourself: *"Do my goals reflect who I really am and what I truly care about?"*

Aligning your goals with passion and purpose begins with knowing what you truly want, followed by discovering what genuinely excites and drives you. You can identify your passion by knowing what you enjoy, what you find yourself doing most of the time, and what makes you happiest when you've done it.

I discovered my passion when I began working in the housing industry. The organization's mission is to provide housing for low-income families by giving rental assistance payments or subsidizing their rent in apartments the organization owned. The stories I heard of families struggling with housing were gut-wrenching. I frequently think how blessed I am not to have to struggle, and because of that, it is important to me to give back.

How many families could I help? I wanted to help all of them! I worked hard to learn everything I could about rental assistance programs and made sure our organization maximized the benefits of these programs. As I found my passion in my work, it wasn't work to me at all. I quickly moved up in the company, from part-time Accounts Payable clerk to Chief Operating Officer.

My success was being in a position to help others find stability in their lives.

Start with what excites you and what gives your life meaning. Then build your goals from there. That way, every step forward feeds both your ambition *and* your soul.

The Moment I Discovered What I Was Actually Working Toward

For years, I thought I had it figured out. I was climbing the ladder. Learning my job inside and out. Becoming excellent at my tasks. Moving from staff accountant to program administration. Earning my master's degree, then pursuing my doctorate.

On paper, I was crushing it. I had goals. I was achieving them. I was becoming the best version of a professional employee. But something was missing. I couldn't name it. I just felt it—a quiet sense that all this striving was leading somewhere, but I wasn't sure where. Or why.

Then I stood in front of a classroom for the first time, and everything changed.

The Setup: Building Credentials, Not Clarity

Let me back up.

After obtaining my master's degree, I made the decision to pursue my doctorate. People asked why, and I gave them the practical answer: "To become a college professor." But the real truth was that I wanted "to make myself so qualified they can't say no."

After being laid off twice, and after facing rejection, I wanted to eliminate every possible excuse an employer could use to overlook me.

But there was something else beneath that motivation; something I couldn't articulate yet.

I was a little over four years into my job—first as a staff accountant, then working in program administration. I was good at what I did. Competent. Reliable. I was the person leadership could count on.

When the COO position opened up, I did something bold: I applied.

Part of me thought, *I may not get this.* I was younger than typical candidates for that level. I didn't have all the traditional experience. But I had credentials now—a master's degree and a doctorate in progress.

And I had a backup plan: *If I don't get this position, I'll be okay. I'm continuing my education. I'm developing my skills. If I can't advance my career here, there's something else for me somewhere else.*

That mindset—that I was building something that transcended any single job or title—gave me confidence to take the leap.

I got the position. I became the Chief Operating Officer.

And I was good at it. Really good. I managed eighty employees across ten offices. I built systems. I led teams. I made decisions that impacted the entire organization.

On paper, this was a success. This was the culmination of all that hard work, all those degrees, all that "dying on the treadmill." But here's the thing: *I still felt like something was missing.*

The Spark: Standing in Front of a Classroom

With my credentials—my master's and my pursuit of the doctorate—I began receiving requests to teach courses in program administration.

At first, I said yes because it seemed like a good professional opportunity. A way to share knowledge. A natural extension of my expertise.

I didn't expect what happened next.

I stood up in front of a room full of strangers—people I'd never met, who knew nothing about me except that I was there to teach them something.

And as I began sharing the knowledge I'd gained over years of work, something inside me ignited.

It wasn't just that I enjoyed it. It was deeper than that.

I felt *alive*.

Every question they asked engaged me. Every concept I explained felt meaningful. Every moment of understanding I saw flash across their faces filled me with a sense of purpose I hadn't felt anywhere else—not even in my COO role.

When the class ended, people approached me.

"That was such a great class. Can I call you if I have questions?"

"This was exactly what I needed. Thank you."

"Would you be willing to mentor me?"

The feeling I had afterward was indescribable. It was joy. It was fulfillment. It was *rightness*.

I thought to myself: *This. This is what I'm supposed to be doing.*

The Realization: Passion Found Me

I began teaching more and more classes. Leadership kept asking, and I kept saying yes—not out of obligation, but because I genuinely loved it. Eventually, I designed a course on my own: **"Growing Your Career."** I poured everything I'd learned—every failure, every lesson, every strategy— into that curriculum. The layoffs. The foreclosure. The doctorate journey. The climb to COO. All of it.

And the course was incredibly well received. Students didn't just attend— they engaged. They opened up. They asked for guidance. They requested that I mentor them beyond the classroom.

That's when the realization hit me with full force:

This is my passion. This is my purpose. This is what I'm supposed to be doing.

Not just being a COO. Not just climbing the corporate ladder. Not just earning degrees and titles.

Teaching. Mentoring. Helping others grow.

I've always had a giving spirit. The most fulfilling part of my COO role wasn't the power or the prestige—it was when I got to help others. Share knowledge.

Watch someone grow because of something I taught them.

I'm also a huge believer that when one teaches, two learn. Every time I explained a concept to someone else, I understood it more deeply myself.

But before this epiphany, I had it all wrong.

What I Thought vs. What I Discovered

What I thought: If I absorb information and learn to do my tasks well, that will fulfill my purpose. That will align with my passion to help others.

What I discovered: All that was really doing was making me a model employee.

And that's great! Being excellent at your job matters. Building skills matters.

Pursuing education matters.

But it wasn't enough.

Being a great employee made me valuable to an organization. But it didn't give me the deep fulfillment I was craving.

I was missing a piece that would bring me peace. That piece? *Alignment.* My goals had been about achievement: get the degree, get the promotion, get the title.

But my passion was about contribution: help others, share knowledge, watch people grow.

My purpose—the reason I'm here, the unique way I'm meant to serve—was always about teaching and mentoring. I just didn't know it until I stood in front of that classroom.

The Difference Alignment Makes

Here's what changed when I finally aligned my goals with my passion and purpose:

Before alignment:

- I was working hard and achieving goals, but something felt off.
- Success felt hollow—like checking boxes instead of living purposefully.
- I was building a career, but not a calling.
- I was competent, but not completely fulfilled.

After alignment:

- Work stopped feeling like work.
- Every class I taught energized me instead of draining me.
- I could see the direct impact of my contribution.

- My goals shifted from "What title can I get?" to "How many people can I help?"
- I finally understood *why* I was pursuing all those credentials—not just to be impressive, but to have knowledge worth sharing. When your goals align with your passion and purpose, everything clicks into place:

You're not just doing—you're becoming.

You're not just achieving—you're contributing.

You're not just successful—you're fulfilled.

The Lesson I Almost Missed

If someone had told me when I started my bachelor's degree in accounting, "You're going to end up being a teacher and mentor," I would have laughed.

Teaching wasn't on my radar. Mentoring wasn't part of my career plan. I was focused on accounting, auditing, program administration—technical skills, not people development.

But passion doesn't always announce itself upfront. Sometimes it jumps out and surprises you.

I thought my purpose was to be excellent at accounting. Then program administration. Then executive leadership. And those were all part of the journey. But they weren't the destination.

My real purpose was always about helping others grow.

Accounting was just one way to do it. Program administration was another.

Executive leadership was another.

But teaching? Mentoring? That was its purest expression.

How to Know When You've Found Alignment

You might be wondering: *How do I know if my goals are aligned with my passion and purpose?*

Here's what I learned.

You've found alignment when:

1. *The work energizes you instead of draining you.*

    Even when I was tired, teaching filled me up. That's not normal— most work depletes us.

2. *You lose track of time.*

Hours in the classroom felt like minutes. That's flow. That's alignment.

3. *People seek you out for more.*

   When students asked to be mentored, it wasn't because I was perfect—it was because they felt the authenticity of someone operating in their purpose.

4. *You'd do it even if no one paid you.*

   I taught extra classes not for money or recognition, but because I genuinely loved it.

5. *It feels like you're becoming who you were always meant to be.*

   Standing in front of that classroom felt like coming home to myself.

You're misaligned when:

1. *Success feels empty.*

   You check the boxes, get the promotion, earn the degree—and feel nothing.

2. *You're constantly exhausted.*

   Not just physically tired, but soul-tired. Depleted in a way rest doesn't fix.

3. *You're good at it but don't love it.*
   Competence isn't the same as calling.
4. *You keep asking, "Is this it?"*
   That nagging feeling that there must be something more.
5. *Your achievements don't satisfy you.*
   You hit the goal and immediately start chasing the next one, never feeling fulfilled.

The Question That Changes Everything

After I discovered teaching and mentoring were my true passion and purpose, I started asking myself a different question.

Before, I asked: *"What do I want to achieve?"* Now, I ask: *"How do I want to contribute?"* That shift changed everything.

My goals are no longer just about titles and credentials. They're about impact.

- How many people can I help?
- How much knowledge can I share?

- How many lives can I influence for the better?

My master's degree and doctorate aren't just accomplishments on my resume anymore. They're tools that make me better at serving my purpose— teaching and mentoring others.

My COO role isn't just a job title. It's a platform that allows me to help eighty employees grow, develop, and succeed. Everything I've built now serves something bigger than just my own advancement.

That's what alignment feels like.

Your Turn: Finding Your Alignment

I can't tell you what your passion and purpose are. That's your work to do. But I can tell you this: *If you feel like something's missing, even when you're achieving goals— pay attention to that feeling.*

It's not ingratitude. It's not weakness. It's not being unrealistic. *It's your soul telling you that achievement without alignment is empty.*

And here's the good news: The clues to your passion and purpose are already in your life.

For me, it was the moment I stood in front of that classroom. The spark I felt.

The energy it gave me. The requests I received for mentoring.

For you, it might be:

- The task at work you do for free because you love it
- The volunteer work that doesn't feel like work
- The topic you can talk about for hours without getting tired
- The moment someone says, "You're so good at this—have you thought about doing it professionally?"
- The thing you do that makes you lose track of time
  Those are breadcrumbs. Follow them.

Now I Continue to Learn

Here's what I know now that I didn't know then:

Striving to be the best version of myself only brings fulfillment when my goals align with my passion and purpose.

I continue to learn. I continue to develop skills. I continue to pursue excellence. But now, it's not just about being a model employee or earning credentials.

It's about becoming a better teacher. A better mentor. A better servant to the people I'm meant to help.

That alignment brings me peace. Not because everything is perfect. Not because I've "arrived." But because I finally know *why* I'm working so hard. It's not for titles or money or status. *It's to help others become the best versions of themselves.* And that—finally—is enough.

Step #4: Believe That You Can

Knowing you can begins with believing you can. If you don't have cheerleaders in your life, you'll need to cheer for yourself. Remember, take 100 percent responsibility for your own life.

It can be challenging—there will be obstacles to overcome—yet it won't be impossible. Trust yourself a little each day and watch how you'll naturally begin to believe that you can. That will be the moment of the mindset shift you need to be successful.

I included a quote from the poem "Our Deepest Fear" at the beginning of this book because many times, doubt comes from fear—whether it's the fear of failure or, contrarily, the fear that you will be great. Then regret sets in and you think, *"Why didn't I do this sooner?"*

Either way, don't let this stop you from believing you can. Being your best self is all about stepping out in faith.

The Job Rejection That Led to a Doctorate

People ask me why I pursued a doctorate. I usually give them the easy answer:

"I wanted to be a college professor."

It's true, but it's not the whole truth.

The real reason? *I wanted to eliminate every possible excuse they could use to reject me.*

Let me take you back to one of the lowest moments of my life.

I was working a job I absolutely loved. I woke up excited to go to work. I felt valued, capable, and on track. Life was good—better than good. I was recently engaged and in the middle of planning my wedding. Everything was falling into place. Then I was laid off.

I remember sitting in that office, hearing the words but not really processing them. It felt surreal. When I got to my car, the tears came. Not just a few tears—ugly, heaving sobs. Real heartbreak.

I wasn't just losing a job. I was losing my identity, my security, and worst of all—my confidence.

The thoughts came fast and cruel:
- What if I can't find another job before the wedding?
- What if I have to get married while unemployed?
- What will people think?
- What if my fiancé loves me less because I'm not successful anymore?

That last thought was the worst. I know now how irrational it was—he never wavered, never made me feel less than. But in that moment, my worth felt tied to my employment status. If I wasn't working, was I even valuable?

I spiraled down a dark tunnel of self-doubt.

I did what you're supposed to do. I updated my resume. I applied for jobs— hundreds of them—every position I thought I was qualified for. Some I wasn't even qualified for, but I applied anyway out of desperation.

I waited for the calls.

A few came. Maybe four or five interviews out of hundreds of applications. I prepared meticulously. I dressed perfectly. I gave what I thought were strong interviews. Then . . . nothing. No callbacks. No offers. Just silence.

With each rejection—or worse, each non-response—a question grew louder in my head:

"Why am I not good enough?"
I had a bachelor's degree. Wasn't that supposed to mean something? I'd spent thousands of dollars and years of my life earning it. I'd graduated. I'd done everything right.

And yet, doors kept closing in my face.

The frustration was suffocating. I checked my email obsessively. Refreshed job boards constantly. Jumped every time my phone rang, only to sink when it wasn't an employer.

Wedding planning that should have been joyful became a source of anxiety. Every vendor meeting, every deposit, I thought: **I'm spending money I might not be able to replace.**

The disappointment wasn't just about unemployment. It was deeper than that. It was about realizing that my degree—the thing I'd invested so much in—apparently wasn't enough. I wasn't enough.

But then something shifted.

Maybe it was hitting rock bottom. Maybe it was exhaustion from the spiral.

Maybe it was finally getting tired of feeling powerless.

Whatever it was, the disappointment ignited something in me.

A question formed: ***"What if I made myself so undeniably qualified that they can't say no?"***

Not just qualified. Overqualified. So educated, so credentialed, so knowledgeable that rejection wouldn't make sense.

I started researching. What did the positions I wanted require? Bachelor's degree—check, I had that. But what about the people who actually got those jobs? What did they have that I didn't?

Experience, yes. But also—advanced degrees. Master's degrees. Some even had doctorates.

I remember the exact moment I looked at doctoral programs. I thought it was crazy at first. Me? A doctorate? I'd barely survived my bachelor's degree.

But then I thought: ***Why not me?***

Who was I not to pursue the highest level of education possible? Who was I not to invest in myself the way I wanted employers to invest in me?

Who was I not to become the most qualified candidate in the room? The voice in my head that had been saying, **"You're not good enough,"** started to quiet down. A new voice emerged: **"You could be more than enough."**

I didn't enroll in a doctoral program immediately. First, I needed a job—any job—to pay the bills. I took positions I was overqualified for. I worked my way up, gaining experience while keeping my eye on the bigger goal.

And when I was finally in a stable position, I enrolled in a master's program. People thought I was crazy. "You're working full-time, married with a child, and going back to school? That's too much."

Maybe it was too much. But I was done making excuses for why I wasn't where I wanted to be. I was done accepting "not enough" as my reality. When I finished my master's, I didn't stop. I enrolled in the doctoral program. "Why do you need a doctorate?" they asked. I then would answer, "To be a college professor." Now, as I've grown mentally and professionally, I respond with, "Because I refuse to give anyone a reason to say no to me."

The doctorate wasn't easy. There were nights I cried from exhaustion. Moments I doubted I could finish. Times I questioned if it was worth the sacrifices.

But every time I wanted to quit, I remembered that version of me sitting in my car after being laid off—sobbing, feeling worthless.

I remembered the silence after job applications. The rejection without explanation. The feeling of not being good enough.

And I thought: **Never again.**

I refused to let circumstances dictate my worth. I refused to let rejection define my capabilities. I refused to let my confidence be dependent on someone else saying yes to me.

Instead, I would become so excellent, so prepared, so credentialed that my value would be undeniable—not just to others, but to myself.

Here's what I learned about believing in myself:

Belief doesn't come from affirmations or positive thinking alone. *It comes from building evidence.*

Every class I completed added to my evidence.

Every paper I wrote proved I could do hard things.

Every obstacle I overcame built my confidence brick by brick.

By the time I earned that doctorate, I didn't just have the credentials. I had unshakable proof that I could commit to something difficult and see it through. That I could be told "this is too hard" and do it anyway. That I could face my own self-doubt and win.

The doctorate wasn't really about the degree. It was about becoming someone who believes she can.

And now, when I apply for a position, I don't apply hoping they'll think I'm good enough. I apply knowing I am more than good enough.

Not because I'm perfect. Not because I have all the answers. But because I've done the work to eliminate every excuse—theirs and mine.

The Question That Changes Everything

When I was unemployed and applying for jobs, I asked: *"Why am I not good enough?"*

That question kept me small, kept me powerless, kept me waiting for someone else to validate my worth.

The question that changed my life was: *"Why not me?"*

That question put the power back in my own hands. It moved me from victim to victor. It transformed rejection from a dead end into a detour toward something better.

So, let me ask you the question that might change your life:

Why not you?

Why can't you pursue that goal?

Why can't you achieve that dream?

Why can't you become the most qualified person in your field? Why can't you earn that degree, start that business, write that book, make that change?

The only honest answer is: *You can.*

Maybe not today. Maybe not even this year. But you can.

The question isn't whether you're capable. The question is whether you're willing to do what it takes to build the evidence that proves it—to yourself first, and then to everyone else.

I earned a doctorate not because I was naturally brilliant. I earned it because I refused to accept "not good enough" as my story.

What story are you ready to refuse?
What evidence are you ready to build?
What version of yourself are you ready to become?

I promise you this: The person who can achieve your goals already exists. It's you. You just have to believe it—and then do the work to prove it.

Step #5: Die on the Treadmill

Wait . . . I need to die before I can be successful? No—that's not what this means at all.

"Die on a treadmill" is a powerful metaphor for relentless work ethic and unshakable commitment. It comes from a famous Will Smith quote:

"If we get on a treadmill together, one of two things is going to happen: you're getting off first, or I'm going to die. It's really that simple."

Dying on a treadmill is about committing yourself to excellence. It is having the discipline and dedication to push through challenges, no matter how hard it gets. If you want to win, you have to make up your mind that you won't stop until the goal has been accomplished.

The most talented individuals have failed to complete goals, but why, if they're so talented? Because they gave up. There was no persistence, no commitment, discipline, or dedication.

I've been successful in my life because I didn't give up on my goals. Even if I had to start over again and again, I stuck with it. When faced with obstacles, I pivoted and kept going. Tired, weak, frustrated, and sabotaged—through it all, I persevered.

Again, your life is up to you. You don't quit. You outlast. You stay on that treadmill until either you win or you pass out trying. That's the mindset.

The Two Times I Did Everything Right—and Lost Anyway

Let me tell you about the two times I died on the treadmill—and the treadmill was pulled out from under me.

The First Time: The Job I Loved

I had found my dream job. Working as an auditor at an insurance audit firm, I was convinced this was it—my career, my future, my path.

I was so certain that I enrolled in a bachelor's degree program in accounting to build my career in the industry. This wasn't just a job to me. This was my trajectory.

And I gave it everything. I mean *everything*.

I arrived early. Stayed late. Worked weekends. I pushed myself to complete as many audits as possible, not because I had to, but because I wanted to be the best. I didn't just meet expectations—I obliterated them.

When new hires came in, I was the one who trained them. Management trusted me with their newest employees because they knew I'd do it right.

I was the definition of a stellar employee. The kind every company says they want. Dedicated. Driven. Excellent.

I was on that treadmill, running hard, refusing to stop. I was doing exactly what you're supposed to do: show up, work hard, prove your worth. My hard work finally paid off. I was promoted to Division Supervisor, a few months after, our firm was bought out by a larger corporation. I was managing staff who used to be my peers. I had arrived! This, of course, came with a substantial pay raise. I bought a new vehicle and my first home. A year later, the larger corporation decided to close our office.

Just like that, it was over.

Not because I wasn't good enough. Not because I didn't work hard enough. Not because I did anything wrong.

I did everything right.

And I still lost my job.

I picked myself up. I found another position at an auto auction, this time as a staff accountant. It wasn't auditing, but it was accounting, and it fit my career path.

And honestly? I loved it.

Auction days were Thursdays, and they were electric. The crowds. The buyers bidding aggressively on vehicles at the auction block. The sellers anxious for top dollar. The energy was incredible. It was busy, chaotic, and fun.

I threw myself into the work. I learned the business quickly. I supervised Accounts Payable and Accounts Receivable. I became the Controller's "righthand woman"—the person she relied on to keep everything running smoothly.

Once again, I was on that treadmill. Running hard. Refusing to quit. Giving my absolute best.

I thought, *This time will be different. This time, hard work will be rewarded with stability.*

Then the private auto auction owners went public.

And the company was bought out by a larger corporation.

And I was laid off.

Again.

The Defeat

I felt crushed.

Not just disappointed. Not just frustrated. *Defeated.*

Because it wasn't just one time. It was twice. Two jobs I genuinely loved. Two times I had given everything I had. Two times I had been a model employee.

And two times, it didn't matter.

The lesson hit me like a punch to the gut: *No matter how hard you work, no matter how well you perform, you are not guaranteed to remain employed.* That's a brutal truth. One that goes against everything we're told about hard work and dedication and "giving 110 percent."

I had died on that treadmill—twice. And both times, the treadmill had been pulled out from under me anyway.

So, what's the point? If hard work doesn't guarantee success, if excellence doesn't protect you, if doing everything right can still end in loss—why bother?

That's the question that haunted me.

The Realization

It took time, but eventually, I had a different realization: *The treadmill didn't disappear. It just moved.*

Those layoffs weren't the end of my story. They were redirections. Painful, unwanted redirections—but redirections nonetheless.

And here's what I learned: *You lose less from disappointments when you are able to learn from them.*

So I asked myself: *What can I take from this? What did I gain, even though I lost the job?*

The answers became clear:

> From the audit firm, I learned how to train people, how to manage multiple projects, how to push myself beyond what I thought possible.
>
> From the auto auction, I learned a completely different business model, how to handle high-pressure situations, how to be indispensable to leadership.

I had skills now. Transferable skills. Skills that no buyout could take from me. But more than that, I had learned something crucial: *If I wanted to build a career that couldn't be taken away by corporate decisions, I needed to invest in myself—not just in my employer.*

The Shift

From that point forward, I changed my approach.

Instead of just learning the tasks I was hired to do, I concentrated on developing skills and qualifications I could take with me to any job.

If I wanted to be a leader someday—a true executive leader—I would need more than technical skills. I would need:

- Time management
- Organization systems
- Creative problem-solving
- The ability to think outside the box
- Leadership presence

So with each position I held after those layoffs, I didn't just do the work. I built systems. I created desktop manuals—not because I was asked to, but because I saw the value in documentation and process improvement. I found creative ways to complete tasks more efficiently, which allowed me to perform well while

simultaneously developing skills I could use later in executive leadership.

I wasn't just being a good employee anymore. I was building a skillset that no one could lay off.

The Truth about "Dying on the Treadmill"

Here's what I want you to understand about dying on the treadmill: *It doesn't guarantee you'll get what you're working toward.*

I know that's not the motivational message you expected. But it's the truth.

I gave everything to those jobs, and I still lost them.

So does that mean "die on the treadmill" is bad advice? That hard work is pointless?

No.

It means this: *Dying on the treadmill isn't about the outcome. It's about who you become in the process.*

When I was laid off the first time, I was devastated. But I had also become someone who could:

- Handle high volumes of work
- Train others effectively
- Push through difficult projects
- Show up consistently

When I was laid off the second time, I was defeated. But I had also become someone who could:

- Learn new industries quickly
- Earn the trust of leadership
- Manage teams
- Thrive in high-pressure environments

Those layoffs took my jobs. They didn't take my growth.

The Lesson I Wish Someone Had Taught Me

If someone had told me earlier, "You're going to lose jobs you love, no matter how hard you work," I would have been devastated.

But if they'd also told me, "And that's going to make you better, stronger, and more prepared for something even greater," I would have understood. *Dying on the treadmill isn't about never falling off. It's about what you do when the treadmill is pulled out from under you.*

Do you give up? Or do you find another treadmill—a better one, a stronger one, one you build yourself?

After those two layoffs, I stopped putting all my faith in employers and started putting it in myself. I went back to school—not just for a bachelor's, but eventually a master's and then a doctorate. I built skills that transcended any single job or industry. I became someone who could lead, not just follow instructions.

And years later, when I sat in the Chief Operating Officer chair, overseeing eighty employees and ten offices, I realized something:

Those layoffs didn't stop me. They prepared me.

Every skill I developed while "dying on the treadmill" at those jobs became essential in my leadership role. The process documentation I learned to create; I used it to build organizational systems. The efficiency improvements I pioneered; I used them to transform operations. The resilience I built from getting back up after being knocked down; I used it to lead through challenges.

I didn't just survive those layoffs. I used them.

What "Die on the Treadmill" Really Means

Let me redefine this for you, based on what I learned the hard way.

"Die on the treadmill" means:

1. *Give your absolute best, regardless of the outcome.*

   Not because it guarantees success, but because it guarantees growth.

2. *Extract the lesson from every failure.*

   Less is lost when you learn from disappointments.

3. *Invest in yourself, not just your employer.*

   Build skills that are yours, that travel with you, that can't be laid off.

4. *Get back on the treadmill after you fall off.*

   And then another. And another. Until you build your own.

5. *Trust that the process is preparing you for something you can't see yet.*

   Those detours aren't dead ends—they're redirections.

When the Treadmill Is Pulled Out from Under You

If you're reading this and you've just lost something you worked hard for—a job, a relationship, an opportunity—I want you to know:

It's okay to be devastated. It's okay to feel defeated. It's okay to grieve what you lost.

I did. Twice.

But then, when you're ready, ask yourself:

- What did I gain, even though I lost?
- What skills did I develop?
- What did this experience teach me about myself?
- How can I take what I learned and apply it somewhere even better? Because here's the truth those layoffs taught me: *You can do everything right and still not get the outcome you expected.*

But that doesn't mean you did it wrong. It means the outcome wasn't yours to control.

What you can control:
- The effort you give
- The skills you build
- The lessons you extract
- The person you become
- The decision to get back on the treadmill

The Question That Changes Everything

After my second layoff, I stopped asking: *"Why did this happen to me?"* I started asking: *"What is this preparing me for?"* That shift changed everything.

Those layoffs prepared me for executive leadership. They taught me resilience. They forced me to invest in myself. They redirected me toward a doctorate I might never have pursued otherwise. What felt like failure at the time was actually training.

So, if you're on a treadmill right now, giving everything you have, and you're afraid it won't be enough—keep going. Not because it guarantees the outcome you want. But because it guarantees you'll be ready for what comes next, even if you can't see it yet.

And if your treadmill was just pulled out from under you—if you just lost something you worked hard for—get back up. Find another treadmill. Or better yet, build your own. Because the point isn't to never fall off. The point is to keep running, no matter how many times the ground shifts beneath you.

That's what "die on the treadmill" really means. And that's what made me unstoppable.

Your Journey—Practical Application

Moment of Reflection: How You Get Inspired

Throughout your journey, you'll pause for moments of reflection. These moments will allow you to write down your thoughts and build on them as you go.

In this first moment of reflection, discuss how you get inspired. When you wake up earlier than usual, are you looking forward to something? What excites you? What do you repeat over and over?

_____

_____

_____

Let's Continue the Journey:
Walking Through the Five Steps

Every great achievement begins with a single step, and each step forward brings you closer to the life you envision. This journey isn't about rushing to the finish line—it's about embracing growth, learning, and resilience along the way. As you walk through these five steps, think of them as milestones that remind you of your strength, your progress, and your ability to keep moving forward no matter what challenges arise.

Step #1 Exercises: 100 Percent Responsible

Now it's your turn. Let me ask you what my father asked me:

Where in your life are your "expenses" (what you're giving) greater than your "income" (what you're receiving)?

This isn't just about money. This could be:

- Giving more energy to a relationship than you're getting back
- Spending more time on things that don't serve your goals
- Investing in people, jobs, or habits that drain you

Write it down. Face it. Own it.

Then ask yourself: What are my two choices?

Because just like I had to either lose the house or make more money, you have to either accept the loss or change the input.

What will you choose?

And more importantly: *Are you ready to take 100 percent responsibility for that choice?*

Where Are You Today?

When answering this question, be honest with yourself. Where are you in your career, in your relationships with family and friends? Where are you financially, spiritually, emotionally, and mentally? Write down as much or as little as you want and anything that comes to mind.

I love . . .

I am not happy with . . .

My relationships are . . .

I am/am not content with my life because . . .

I wish _____ was better . . .

Why or Why Not?

Review your responses to "Where are you today?" and ask yourself why or why not? List whatever comes to mind.

Are These Excuses?

From your list of whys and why-nots, ask yourself: Are these excuses? How can you overcome them?

If the relationship isn't how you want it, can you talk it out?

If you don't love your job, do you get another one?

_____

_____

_____

_____

By listing your whys and why-nots, you can begin to break them down into how you overcome them. Overcoming is where you begin to take 100 percent responsibility for your own life.

You may have had bad relationships, had your heart broken, or had something stolen from you. How you handle these disappointments and use them as fuel for motivation is taking responsibility. Let me be clear: I'm not minimizing your pain. What happened to you was real. But what happens next is up to you.

You feel you don't have time to study or work out because your spouse, partner, kids, or parents need you for several different things. If you say yes to everything and everyone, this is the schedule you've created. Make sure you're available to yourself and that you set aside time each day just for you.

My personal time is from when I wake up in the morning to the time I leave my bedroom. That is my time because I know as soon as I leave the bedroom, I'm in mommy mode, getting in the car to travel to work, giving my attention to work for the day. Once I leave work, I will be preparing dinner and focusing on family time.

I know what you're thinking: This all seems so simple. You're right, it does! Yet taking 100 percent responsibility for your own life takes practice. It's okay if you don't get it right the first time. If you continue to work on it, it will happen. You'll find yourself wondering why something isn't quite the way you'd like it, then start listing reasons in your head and asking yourself, *How do I overcome this?*

Now that you've examined what you don't like and those things in your life you'd like to change, move on to Step #2: discovering what you want.

Step #2 Exercises: Your Turn—What Do You Really Want?

The exercises that follow will help you peel back the layers of "should" and discover your authentic wants. Be honest. Be brave. Be willing to face what you've been avoiding.

Your real life is waiting.

After you've begun to take 100 percent responsibility for your own life, you can start working toward what you want. Better health? Better relationships? A better career? To be more spiritual?

You can examine this by first understanding what makes you feel good. Figure out what you want by identifying those things you do every day that ignite the passion within you—those things you enjoy repeating.

If you don't know what you want yet, that's okay, but it's your job to find out. Clarity doesn't come from waiting; it comes from exploring. Whether it's a particular activity or task, if you think you'd like it, try it out!

List the Things You Enjoy:

_____
_____
_____
_____
_____
_____

List What You Are Passionate About:

_____
_____
_____
_____
_____
_____

Not Sure What You're Passionate About?

Identify your why! Why do you get out of bed in the morning? Why were you motivated to start this journey? Think of the people in your life—do they make you want to be a better person?

Your Why: *To feel better, To be happier, To create a better life for your children, To develop a better life for yourself*

_____
_____
_____
_____

List What You Would Like to Try

_____
_____
_____
_____

I'm going to ask you some hard questions. The same ones I wish I'd asked myself at age thirty.

Question 1: What are you saying *yes* to because you think you should?

Marriage? A career path? A lifestyle? A relationship? A living situation?

Write it down:

Question 2: Why do you think you should want it?

What voice in your head is telling you this is what you're supposed to choose?

Society? Family? Fear? Pain? Someone else's expectations?

Question 3: If you removed the "should"—what would you actually want? If no one else's opinion mattered, if there were no consequences, if you could design your life exactly as you wanted it—what would it look like?

Question 4: What are you afraid will happen if you admit what you really want?

Judgment? Disappointment? Loneliness? Failure? Loss?

Question 5: What is it costing you to NOT pursue what you actually want?

Time? Energy? Joy? Growth? Your authentic self?

Step #3 Exercises: Align Your Goals with Passion and Purpose

The journey to uncovering your passion and purpose is both exciting and transformative. Along the way, you'll need to explore new experiences and step outside your comfort zone. Passion often points the way to purpose, especially when you recognize how your enthusiasm impacts and uplifts those around you. When you use your talents to brighten someone else's life, you create a powerful alignment between what you love and why you do it. And remember: set goals that truly reflect what matters to you at your core, not just what looks impressive on paper.

Purpose is the reason you journey, and Passion is the fire that lights the way. ~Unknown

Finding Your Passion

Finding your passion is the journey of unraveling what makes your soul come alive—the work, ideas, or causes that energize and challenge you. It's not just about what you're good at, but what you feel called to do, even when no one is watching.

Passion is your inner compass, pointing you toward a life of meaning, impact, and joy.

We spend so much of our lives chasing success, approval, and stability, but what if the most powerful thing we could chase is what sets our soul on fire? Finding your passion isn't about luck. It's about paying attention. It's about listening to the quiet voice inside that says, *"This matters to me."* It's about noticing when you feel most alive and fully present. That's not an accident.

That's a signal.

It can be found in the things you do for free, the topics you bring up in every conversation, the work you'd keep doing even if no one ever gave you a title. And passion isn't just about you. It's about what you give to others when you're lit up from within. Because when you live with passion, you inspire people without even trying. You unlock doors that effort alone could never open.

So, if you haven't found your passion yet, don't panic. Be curious. Explore. Try things. Fail. Try again.

Passion doesn't always arrive fully formed. We build it step by step, by doing the things that feel meaningful, even when no one else understands why. And when you find it, hold on. Feed it. Protect it. Because passion, aligned with purpose, becomes power.

Finding Your Purpose

Finding your purpose is the moment you realize that your life is about more than survival—it's about significance. It's discovering the unique way you're meant to serve, contribute, and make a difference in the world. Purpose is the intersection of your pain, your passion, and your gifts—all working together to leave something better than you found it. It's not just what you do; it's who you're becoming and why it matters.

Finding your purpose isn't about having all the answers. It's about daring to ask the right questions.

Why am I here? What am I meant to do? Does my life have meaning? These aren't just deep thoughts—they're the start of something powerful.

Purpose isn't a job title, a paycheck, or even a goal. Purpose is why you get back up when life knocks you down. It's the fire in your heart that keeps burning, even when no one else sees it. It's what gives your days meaning and your actions weight.

You don't find purpose like a lost key—you build it, moment by moment, by showing up for what matters.

Sometimes, your purpose is hiding in plain sight:
- In the pain you've overcome
- In the joy you give others
- In the quiet, persistent voice that says, *"This is what I'm meant to do"*

Your purpose isn't just about you. It's about how your life touches others— how your story becomes someone else's survival guide. It's the legacy you leave behind, not in monuments or medals, but in people changed because you showed up.

So, if you're still searching, keep going. Explore. Serve. Reflect.

And know this: you don't have to be perfect to be purposeful. You just have to be willing to live with intention.

Because when you live on purpose, you don't just exist. You lead. You lift. You become unstoppable.

Moment of Reflection: My Passion and Purpose

My Passion:
_____
_____
_____
_____
_____

My Purpose:
_____
_____
_____
_____
_____

Based on your identified passion and purpose, where do you need to be to align the two?

What changes will you make in your life in the journey to discovering and fulfilling your passion and purpose?

Exercise: Discovering Your Alignment

Part 1: The Spark Moments

Think about the last time you felt truly alive and energized by something you were doing (work or personal).

What were you doing?

Who were you helping or serving?

How did you feel afterward?

Part 2: Your Hidden Clues

What do people frequently ask you to help them with?

What topic could you talk about for hours?

What would you do even if no one paid you?

Part 3: Achievement vs. Fulfillment

List three achievements you're proud of:

1.

2.

3.

Which of these left you feeling the most fulfilled (not just accomplished)?

What was different about that one?

Part 4: From Achievement to Contribution

Rewrite your current goals from "What do I want to achieve?" to "How do I want to contribute?" Example:

- Achievement goal: "Get promoted to manager"
- Contribution goal: "Develop leadership skills so I can mentor ten people"

Your achievement goals:

Rewritten as contribution goals:

Part 5: Your Purpose Statement

Complete this statement:

"I am at my best when I am

_____

(activity)

for_____

(who)

because_____

(why it matters)."

Example: "I am at my best when I am teaching career development for young professionals because watching them discover their potential gives me purpose."

Your statement:

_____

_____

_____

Remember:

Your goals can take you far. But only aligned goals can take you home—to the version of yourself you were always meant to become.

Keep striving. But make sure you're striving toward something that feeds your soul, not just your résumé. That's when you'll finally bring your best to whatever you do.

Moment of Reflection: How Do You Desire to Express Yourself?

How do you desire to express yourself right now?

Hint: Your expression is your gift.

Step #4 Exercises: Why Not You?

Believe You Can

Have you ever been told you were able to do something? When growing up, your parents may have told you that you can be whatever you want to be.

Then you coast through life doing things for others. You may never discover what it is you want to be. You go through life in survival mode: finish high school, go to college, get married, have kids, buy a house. One day you wake up realizing you lost focus on yourself and what you want to do in life. Then you think, *It's too late now. I have a spouse, kids, a forty-hour-a-week job, and several people who depend on me to do just what I'm doing.*

Yes, it happens to all of us. But it's not too late to go after the life you want. It's never too late to focus on being your best self. That first starts with believing you can.

You've adapted to and become comfortable with the things life has given you. Ask yourself: Am I truly being my best self? Am I bringing my best to whatever I do? If not, this is where the real work comes in. And I do mean work!

In my last semester working on my bachelor's degree, I was taking a full load of college courses, working a full-time job, maintaining a home, and planning a wedding. Talk about having a lot on your plate. Some days I thought, *How am I going to keep going at this pace?* I told myself I must keep going.

One reason was that I wanted to be a college graduate, and I wanted to be a wife and mother. I had to prioritize my days, ensuring I gave attention to my fiancé and focused on my coursework while making it into the office each day and being productive.

Was it hard? Yes, it was. Throughout it all, I sacrificed myself. I forgot to focus on self-care. I was no longer taking moments for myself. No napping, reading, exercising, spa visits, anything that I actually enjoyed. Did it do some damage?

Yes, it did.

I just kept telling myself: *I can do this. Focus now and reap the rewards later.* I believed deep down that I could be all those things. Through the late-night paper writing, early morning studying, cake tasting, and gown shopping, I kept going.

I knew that if I accomplished my college degree, I would be successful.

Now it's your turn to silence the doubt and build the belief.

Exercise: Building Your Evidence

Part 1: What "They" Say You Can't Do

Write down one goal where you've felt "not good enough" or heard (external or internal) voices suggesting you can't:

_____

_____

Part 2: Why Not You?

Answer this honestly: What's actually stopping you? Not excuses—the real obstacles:

Part 3: Evidence You Already Have

List ten things you've already accomplished that prove you can do hard things:

1.
2.
3.
4.
5.
6.
7.

8.

9.

10.

Part 4: Evidence You'll Build

What specific actions will you take to build evidence of your capability?

Example: **"I'll take one certification course in my field."**

Example: **"I'll complete one small project that proves I can finish what I start."**

Your evidence-building actions:

Remember: Belief isn't magic. It's built one piece of evidence at a time.

Start building today.

Part 5: Evaluating Who You Are

Evaluating who you are and what you can do begins with writing everything you are. Remember to be positive! Brag on yourself—you'll love it!

Write "I am" in front of each statement and write as many as you want.

I am smart. *I am kind.*
I am beautiful. *I am loving.*
I am patient. *I am unique.*

You get the idea!

Part 6: Defining Who You Are

Now break it down a little further and define who you are. Pretend someone asked you, *"Who are you?"* What would be your response?

I am a teacher. *I am a mother.*

I am a provider. *I am a nurturer.*

Next, put these lists together to tell who you are in one sentence. For instance, *I am a smart, beautiful mother who is patient, kind, and a great teacher.*

Your gift is something that comes easily to you but is hard for others. ~Mary Anne Radmacher

Part 7: What Can You Do?

Now that you've explored who you are, list what you can do. Pretend you're in a job interview for your dream career choice. How would you let the interviewer know what you can do?

By listing what you can do, you can focus on what you do well and further discover your gift.

Moment of Reflection: How Do You Desire to Express Yourself?

What kind of life do you desire to live? How would your gift play a role in creating that life?

True desire in your heart, for anything good, is God's proof to you, sent beforehand, that it's yours already.
~Denzel Washington

Step #5 Exercises: Die on a Treadmill

The last step I'd like to identify in the journey of my success is Step #5: Die on a treadmill. Now, I don't mean to literally die, but to be so determined to meet your goal that you'll keep pushing yourself until it's done. It takes perseverance, discipline, and consistency.

Discipline is the bridge between goals and accomplishments. ~Jim Rohn

As we discussed earlier, "Die on a treadmill" is a metaphor that means bringing your best will sometimes involve outworking everyone. It's not about being the smartest or the most talented—it's about refusing to quit.

The treadmill symbolizes the grind. The commitment over comfort. I found that I became most powerful when I discovered I was comfortable with the uncomfortable. There will be situations where you'll need to sacrifice the comforts in life, where you'll need to challenge yourself. These situations can be highly uncomfortable. Yet if you remain steadfast and stay on it, no matter how tired, discouraged, or uncertain you feel, you'll develop a mindset of total dedication.

You're so committed to your goal that failure isn't an option. Being your best self requires deep dedication to reach your goals. If you're going to excel, you must be willing to "die on a treadmill."

While working on my doctorate, I was also working a full-time job in a highly responsible executive position with eighty employees, ten offices, over twenty entities . . . you get the picture!

I was a single mother of a teenager and taking care of a household, parents, siblings, and friends. In the midst of it all, I needed to find time for self-care. Needless to say, I was tired. I had moments when I wanted to give up. I doubted my ability to complete simple tasks daily. Yet I knew I could not quit! That took both discipline and consistency, and most importantly, it took dedication.

How? I established my why: I wanted to make my parents proud, and I wanted to show my son persistence and resilience.

As long as I had breath, I was going to reach my goal! When moments were tough, I kept telling myself, *"Die on a treadmill."*

Exercise: When the Treadmill Was Pulled Out from Under You

Part 1: Your "Treadmill Moments"

Think of a time you gave your best effort and still didn't get the outcome you wanted.

What was it?

How did you feel when it didn't work out?

Part 2: What You Gained

Even though you didn't get what you were working toward, what did you gain?

Skills:

Lessons:

Strengths:

Part 3: The Redirection

Looking back, how did that "failure" redirect you toward something better?

What opportunity came *because* of that loss?

Part 4: Skills for Your Next Treadmill

Based on what you learned, what skills will you develop that no one can take from you?

1.
2.
3.
4.
5.

Part 5: Your Commitment

Complete this statement:

"*Even if the outcome isn't guaranteed, I will keep 'dying on the treadmill' because* _____."

Remember:

Dying on the treadmill doesn't guarantee you'll reach your destination. It guarantees you'll be stronger when you get there—wherever "there" turns out to be.

Keep running.

Creating Your Plan

Setting Goals for Success

Set five-year goals and then break them down to annual, monthly, and weekly goals. Your goals should be written in a way that allows you to align your passion and purpose.

For instance: My passion is teaching and mentoring. My purpose is to help others, to take what I learn and give that knowledge to someone else. My five-year goal is to become a professor. My annual goal is to get my credentials, degrees, certifications, and research.

Breaking down your goals like this allows you to make sure you're on track and to revise if there's a need for a pivot in your plan. And that's okay!

Five-Year Goals

Where do you want to be at the end of five years? What do you see in your life moving forward?

Annual Goals

Each year, completing goals toward your five-year goal keeps you on track!

Monthly Goals

Monthly goals need to be identified so that you know your daily goals are being met.

Weekly Goals

What can you do each week toward your annual goals?

Dreams without goals are just dreams, and ultimately, they fuel disappointment. ~Denzel Washington

Using Your Monthly Calendar

The following pages provide a monthly calendar template to help you track your progress toward your monthly goals. Here's how to use it effectively:

At the beginning of each month:

1. Write your monthly goal at the top
2. Break it down into daily action steps
3. Write what you'll do each day to move closer to your goal Check-in points:

- Week 2 (around day 8): Are you on track?
- Week 3 (around day 15): Are you still on track? If not, what can you shift? Revisit your purpose and passion
- Week 4 (around day 22): Final push! You're almost there!

At the end of the month:

Celebrate your progress.

Reflect on what worked and what didn't.

Set your goal for the next month.

Remember: This is your journey. Adjust as needed, but never give up.

Monthly Calendar Template

Monthly Goal: _____

Week 1

Day 1:

Day 2:

Day 3:

Day 4:

Day 5:

Day 6:

Day 7:

Check-in: Are you on track to complete your monthly goal?

Week 2

Day 8:

Day 9:

Day 10:

Day 11:

Day 12:

Day 13:

Day 14:

Check-in: Are you on track to complete your monthly goal?

Week 3

Day 15:

Day 16:

Day 17:

Day 18:

Day 19:

Day 20:

Day 21:

Check-in: One week left! So proud of you! Pat yourself on the back. At this point, you should feel much more empowered!

Final Days

Day 22:

Day 23:

Day 24:

Day 25:

Day 26:

Day 27:

Day 28:

Day 29 (if applicable):

Day 30 (if applicable):

Day 31 (if applicable):

End of Month Reflection

What did I accomplish this month?

What challenged me?

What will I do differently next month?

My goal for next month is:

Conclusion: Your Journey Begins Now

You've made it to the end of this book, but really, you're standing at the beginning. The beginning of a life lived with intention. The beginning of becoming your best self. The beginning of bringing excellence to whatever you do. When I sat in that studio apartment at age twenty-three, feeling stuck in mediocrity, I couldn't have imagined where this journey would take me. From barely graduating high school to earning a doctorate. From feeling purposeless to helping families find stable housing. From existing to truly living. But here's what I want you to understand: *My story isn't special because of what I achieved. It's special because I refused to stay where I was.*

And that's exactly what you're doing right now by working through this book.

The Five Steps Revisited

Let me remind you one more time of the framework that changed my life:

Step #1: Be 100 Percent Responsible for Your Own Life

Stop blaming. Start owning. Your life is yours to shape.

Step #2: Discover What You Want

Get clear. Get honest. Get specific about your desires.

Step #3: Align Your Goals with Your Passion and Purpose

Make sure every goal feeds your soul, not just your resume.

Step #4: Believe That You Can

Trust yourself. Cheer for yourself. Step out on faith.

Step #5: Die on the Treadmill

Commit fully. Outlast the obstacles. Refuse to quit.

What Happens Next?

In this book, I've shared some personal stories. I did that to show you that you too can develop a growth mindset no matter how difficult life gets. Together, these stories show:

- Financial crisis → Responsibility
- Personal crisis → Self-discovery
- Emotional crisis → Alignment

- Professional crisis → Self-belief
- Career setbacks → Resilience & skill-building

Success isn't a destination; it's a practice. It's what you do tomorrow morning when the alarm goes off. It's the choice you make when you're tired. It's the moment you decide to try one more time.

Some days you'll feel unstoppable. Other days you'll question everything.

Both are part of the journey. What matters is that you keep going.

Use the tools in this book:

- The reflection prompts to understand yourself
- The goal-setting templates to create your roadmap
- The monthly calendars to track your progress
- The five steps to guide your decisions

But most importantly, use your story—the one you're writing right now—to remind yourself that you're capable of more than you ever imagined.

My Final Words to You

I started this book with Marianne Williamson's words: "Our deepest fear is not that we are inadequate. Our deepest fear is that we are powerful beyond measure."

So, let me ask you: Who are you not to be great?

You have everything you need within you right now. The passion. The purpose. The power. All that's left is the decision to pursue it relentlessly. Your best self is waiting. Your best life is calling. Your best work is ready to be done. So, get up. Show up. And bring your absolute best to whatever you do. Because the world needs what only you can give. And one day, someone will read your story and think, "If they did it, so can I." Let that someone be inspired by you.

Now go. Your journey awaits!

"The meaning of life is to find your gift. The purpose of life is to give it away." — Often attributed to Pablo Picasso

About the Author

Dr. Lashun Bland's life is a testament to the power of refusing to stay stuck.

Born in Arkansas, Dr. Bland was raised in London, England, from age one to eight. When she returned to Jacksonville, Arkansas—a town of approximately 36,000 people—she always felt like a big-city girl trapped in a small town. That feeling of being meant for more would become the driving force behind everything she accomplished.

At twenty-three, she sat in her studio apartment, preparing for another day at a job she called "mediocre," and made the decision: she wanted to live, not just exist. That moment of clarity sparked a transformation that would take her from receiving foreclosure notices to earning a Doctorate of Business Administration; from navigating financial crisis to becoming Chief Operating Officer, and from self-doubt to an unshakable purpose.

But the path wasn't linear or easy. Along the way, Dr. Bland has been laid off twice, navigated personal setbacks, worked three jobs simultaneously to save her home, and discovered that true success isn't about never falling—it's about what you build while getting back up.

She's made decisions she later had to undo. She's questioned her worth, her capabilities, and whether any of it was worth the struggle.

The answer, she discovered, is *yes*—but only when your goals align with your true purpose.

Today, Dr. Bland splits her passion between executive leadership and education. While managing multiple offices and entities as COO, she also teaches courses in career development and mentors professionals who are ready to stop settling and start thriving. Her course "Growing Your Career" has become a catalyst for countless career transformations.

She believes deeply that where you start doesn't determine where you finish—the only thing that matters is what you do with what you're given. She is a mother, mentor, and believer that when one teaches, two learn. Dr. Bland lives in Arkansas with her son, who keeps her grounded in what truly matters: showing up, even when it's hard.

Bringing Your Best to Whatever You Do is her first book—but certainly not her last lesson in resilience.

www.ingramcontent.com/pod-product-compliance
Lightning Source LLC
Chambersburg PA
CBHW071129090426
42736CB00012B/2066